T2-BVN-148

Native Americans

Tlingit Indians

Suzanne Morgan Williams

Heinemann Library
Chicago, Illinois

Photo research by Alan Gottlieb
Maps by John Fleck
Production by Que-Net Media

07 06 05
10 9 8 7 6 5 4 3 2

Library of Congress Cataloging-in-Publication Data
Williams, Suzanne, 1949-
    Tlingit Indians / Suzanne Morgan Williams.
        v. cm. -- (Native Americans)
Includes bibliographical references and index.
Contents: Southeast Alaska -- Traveling to the sea -- The Ravens and the Eagles -- Villages and clans -- Living from the land and sea -- Clan art -- A Tlingit year -- Celebrations -- New people -- Sickness and change -- Taking land and treasures -- Alaska Native Brotherhood -- Modern and traditional -- The Tlingit future.
    ISBN 1-4034-0868-8 (lib. bdg.) -- ISBN 1-4034-4176-6 (pbk.)
    1. Tlingit Indians--Juvenile literature. [1. Tlingit Indians. 2. Indians of North America--Alaska.] I. Title. II. Native Americans (Heinemann Library (Firm))
    E99.T6W56 2003
    979.8004'972--dc21

                                        2003007477

Acknowledgments
The author and publisher are grateful to the following for permission to reproduce copyright material:
pp. 4, 5 ©Macduff Everton/Corbis; p. 6 Kim Heacox/The Image Bank/Getty Images; p. 7 Barbara Brundage/Accent Alaska; p. 8 American Museum of Natural History Library/Neg.#338688; p. 9 Christie's Images/Corbis; p. 10 Alaska State Library/Neg.#PCA 87-1; p. 11 Alaska State Library/Neg.#PCA 87-10; p. 12 MCSUA/University of Washington Libraries/Neg#NA3945; p. 13 Alaska State Library/Neg.#PCA 87-106; p. 14 MCSUA/University of Washington Libraries/Neg#NA3854; p. 15 Burstein Collection/Corbis; p. 16 Alaska State Library/Neg.#PCA 87-197; pp. 17, 19 American Museum of Natural History Library/Photo by Emmons/Neg.#338436s; p. 18 Courtesy of the Bancroft Library/University of California, Berkleley; p. 20 Alaska Sate Library/Neg.#PCA 20-143; p. 21 Kennan Ward/Corbis; p. 22 MCSUA/University of Washington Libraries/Neg#NA2192; p. 23 MCSUA/University of Washington Libraries/Neg#NA2506; p. 24 David Muench/Corbis; p. 25 Alaska State Library/Neg.# PCA 20-98; p. 26 Courtesey Sheldon Jackson College/Stratton Library; p. 27 Alaska S tate Library/Neg.#PCA 274-1-2; p. 28 Jennifer Ortiz/Tundra Times Photograph Project/Tuzzy Consortium Library; p. 29 Jon Chase/Harvard News Office, © 2001 President and Fellows of Harvard College.; p. 30 Mark Kelley

Cover photograph by Vince Streano/Corbis

Special thanks to Mark (Hans) Chester and Roy Iutzi-Mitchell for their help in the preparation of this book.

Every effort has been made to contact copyright holders of any material reproduced in this book. Any omissions will be rectified in subsequent printings if notice is given to the publisher.

Some words are shown in bold, **like this.** You can find out what they mean by looking in the glossary.

Contents

Southeast Alaska

A bear walks along a stream. The stream spreads out and flows to the beach. Waves wet the stones and rocks along the shore. They shine in the late afternoon sun. Three **killer whales** jump and dive in the sea. **Ravens** squawk from a **cedar** tree. The bear moves toward the forest, looking for berries to eat.

This is southeast Alaska. Tlingit Indians live here and in the northwest part of Canada. Their **ancestors** learned to live in the mountains, in the forest, and by the sea. The Tlingit people are a part of this place.

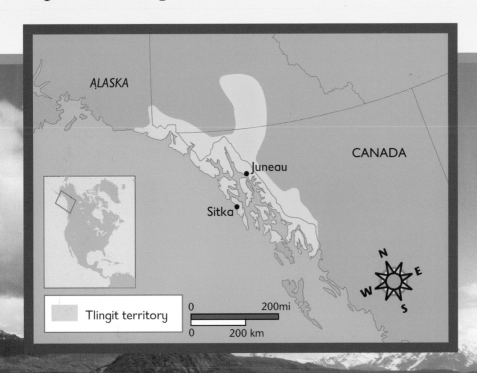

ALASKA

CANADA

Juneau

Sitka

Tlingit territory

0   200mi

0   200 km

N
W   E
S

Traveling to the Sea

Tlingit people say they came to southeast Alaska
a long time ago. Thousands of years ago, ice
covered much of present-day Alaska. Tlingits lived
in the mountains, far away from the sea. They heard
about a place with many fish. They decided to go
there. They walked for a long time. Finally, they came
to a huge **glacier.** No one knew how to cross it.

There are thousands of glaciers in the state of Alaska.

The tunnel under the glacier might have looked like this.

Then they found a tunnel under the glacier. A
river ran beneath the ice, but it looked dangerous.
Four old women offered to help. They paddled a
boat under the glacier and came out safely on the
other side. Then the Tlingits knew the way was safe.
They continued toward their new home by the sea.

The Ravens
and the Eagles

Tlingit people lived, worked, and traveled in **clans**. Clans are groups of relatives who help each other. A clan is a big family. Tlingit clans are divided into two groups, called **moieties**. The moieties are named **Ravens** and Eagles. When Tlingit children are born, they become part of their mother's clan and moiety.

Introductions
It is polite to introduce Tlingit people with their Tlingit name, moiety, and clan.

Clan hats tell what clan Tlingits are a part of.
The people in this 1895 photograph are at a celebration.

8

*Tlingits **carve** many objects. This is a wood rattle in the shape of a raven.*

In the past, Ravens married Eagles. Eagles married Ravens. Tlingits never married someone from their own moiety. Ravens and Eagles did certain jobs for each other. They helped when a family needed a new house or when someone died. Clans and moieties are still important to the Tlingits. But the rules about marriage and jobs are not always followed today.

Villages and Clans

Tlingits say that long ago when they reached their new home by the sea, different **clans** went in different directions. They built villages all along the coast. Men built clan houses with boards made from **cedar** or other trees. Each clan lived in its own large house. If the house got too crowded, some people built a new one.

*This photograph of a Tlingit village was taken in 1895. Some of the houses are **traditional**, and some are modern.*

*Some Tlingit houses were very big. This is the house of a Tlingit leader. The **carvings** show **clan symbols** and stories.*

When Tlingits married, someone had to move. The wife moved into her husband's clan house. Soon, members of many clans lived in each village. Tlingit travelers were welcomed at their clan's house in other villages.

In Their Own Words

"Cousins from the same **moiety** call each other brother and sister. They are very close. There is never anyone who is alone."

—Mark (Hans) Chester of the Coho Clan from the Far Out by the Ocean House, Frog House, Tlingit, 2002

Living from the Land and Sea

Tlingits got everything they needed from the land and sea. Men hunted seals and sea otters, and they caught fish. They hunted deer, rabbits, and bears. Men **carved canoes** from **cedar** trees. Women cooked berries and other foods. They **wove** baskets, clothing, and rain hats. Women also prepared animal skins for clothes. Some families had **slaves** who had been taken from other **tribes.** They helped with this work.

Tlingits were good traders. They used large canoes like this one to travel in the ocean. This picture was made in 1786.

*These Tlingit women are weaving baskets from the roots of **spruce** trees.*

The Tlingit people also had time to make beautiful things. They decorated their houses, canoes, and clothing with **clan symbols. Clans** owned many things. Each clan owned its houses and a fishing area. Clans call the important things they own *at.óow. At.óow* are used in clan celebrations.

In Their Own Words

"We are as one with our **ancestors** and children. We are as one with the land and animals."

—Rosita Worl of the Shangukeidi Clan from the House Lowered from the Sun, Tlingit, 1997

Clan Art

Tlingit artists create *at.óow,* or things that are important to the **clans.** A clan leader might ask an artist to **carve** a **totem pole.** He asks that the totem pole tell a story or something about the clan's history. Some women make *chilkat* **weavings.** They weave **cedar** bark and wool into clothing. *Chilkat* weavings are used for **ceremonies.**

Many people work together to carve a totem pole. This photograph was taken in 1939.

The Tlingit Bear clan's leader wore this hat. You can see the bear clan symbol.

Totem poles and weavings are decorated with **clan symbols.** Only clan members can use the symbols. Each symbol has a story or meaning. Today, Tlingit carvers and weavers are known around the world.

Clan Names

Clans are named by where they are from. Clan symbols are often birds, fish, or animals. They are written here in English and Tlingit.

Beaver	*Deisheetaan*
Killer Whale	*Da<u>k</u>l'aweidí*
Wolf	*Kaagwaantaan*

A Tlingit Year

Today, as in the past, Tlingit children learn all year long by watching and doing. Boys learn from their uncles. Girls learn from their grandmothers, mothers, and aunts. Many Tlingit people still hunt and fish for part of their food. In the spring, Tlingits hunt seals. They also catch fish. They fix hunting gear and tools.

This woman is **weaving** a chilkat **robe.** Most of the weaving was done in the winter.

This 1889 photograph shows a Tlingit summer fishing camp. The fish were hung up on racks to dry.

In the summer, families often move to hunting or fishing camps. They catch salmon and hunt. Women and children pick berries and gather eggs. Today, Tlingits have jobs and go to school. This means that now they may go to their camps on weekends or for vacations. In the past, winter was a time for **ceremonies,** storytelling, and getting together in the villages.

Celebrations

A celebration called a *koo.éex'* helps Tlingits remember important things. In the past, it was also an important way for the **clans** to share things they owned. Some Tlingit families were rich and others were not. Powerful Tlingit clan leaders shared with everyone at a *koo.éex'*.

Tlingit Women

Clan women passed clan knowledge to their daughters. The clan leaders were the sons of important women in the clan.

Tlingits dressed up for koo.éex' celebrations. Many times these celebrations honored a marriage or a death.

Chilkat **robes** are worn at gatherings such as ḵoo.éex'. This photo was taken in 1901.

One clan held the ḵoo.éex', but the whole village came. Clan members from other villages came, too. Clans gave away many gifts. Everyone danced, ate, and listened to stories. People were honored, buried, or married at a ḵoo.éex'. The guests' job was to remember what happened.

New People

Tlingits say that the first white people came to southeast Alaska in the 1770s. Traders came from Russia, England, Spain, and the United States. They wanted furs from sea otters and other animals. Russian traders built **forts** near the Tlingits. But the Tlingits did not want Russians on the land. In 1802, many Tlingits fought the Russians. They destroyed a Russian fort at Sitka.

This 1805 painting shows Sitka. It was one of the first towns that Russians built on Tlingit lands.

Sea otter furs are very soft. They were worth a lot to traders.

In 1804, Russians attacked the Tlingits who lived near the fort. These Tlingits walked many days to a new camp. They told other Tlingit people not to trade with the Russians. In 1805, another group of Tlingits destroyed a Russian fort near their village.

Sickness and Change

Things changed after traders and missionaries came to Alaska. Europeans brought new **diseases** to Tlingit villages. Many Tlingits died from these diseases. The Russians and Europeans got sick and died, too. Others were killed in battles or decided to go home. Many missionaries stayed. They wanted the Tlingits to become **Christians**.

Family Names

Missionaries from the United States called Tlingit families by new names such as Tom, Paul, or Fred. Today many Tlingit families have these kinds of last names.

These Tlingit men and women worked for a fishing company. The photograph was taken around 1908.

This photo of Tlingit children was taken at an Indian boarding school around 1888.

In 1867 the United States paid Russia for the land where Tlingits and other native groups lived. This became the state of Alaska. People from the United States came. They built towns, **canneries,** and lumber camps near Tlingit villages. The United States government sent Tlingit children to **boarding school.** The children had to speak English and wear European-style clothes. The government did not let Tlingits have *koo.éex'* **ceremonies.** Tlingit life was changed.

Taking Treasures

Tlingits shared the land. But in the 1880s, the United States government divided up Tlingit land. It gave or sold the land to single owners. Some Tlingits got land. But it was not as much land as they needed to live on. Many Tlingits did not get any land. The government sold some land to lumber companies, businesses, and miners. In 1902 the United States government took more Tlingit land. The government created the Tongass National Forest. Tlingits could not use that land, either.

*Later, the United States government paid Alaskan **tribes** for the land in the Tongass National Forest.*

24

Collectors took at.óow, totem poles, and clan house decorations from villages like this one.

In the 1890s and early 1900s, scientists and art collectors visited southeast Alaska. In the summer, Tlingits were away from their villages at summer fishing camps. The collectors thought that no one lived there. They took *at.óow,* **totem poles,** and **clan** house decorations to far-away museums and universities.

Alaska Native Brotherhood

In 1912 leaders from the Tlingits and other Alaskan tribes formed the Alaska Native Brotherhood. They wanted to help their people learn to live with the changes. They thought the people in their tribes should learn English. Leaders hoped this would help their people work with **settlers.** Many Tlingits stopped teaching the Tlingit language to their children.

The Alaska Native Brotherhood and Sisterhood work for the rights of Indians. This photograph was taken around 1914.

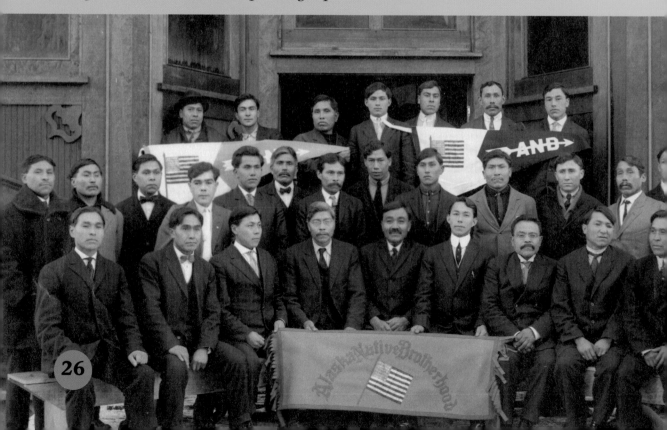

The governor of Alaska signed the state's anti-discrimination law in 1945. Elizabeth Peratrovich is second from the left in this picture.

White settlers did not always treat Indians fairly. They did not let Alaskan natives send their children to public schools or use certain hotels and restaurants. Elizabeth Wanamaker Peratrovich was a Tlingit. She belonged to the Alaska Native Sisterhood. She pushed the Alaska state government to pass an **anti-discrimination law.** The law opened restaurants, hotels, and housing to Alaskan natives. It was the first law like this in the United States.

Modern and Traditional

Today's Tlingit people speak English. They work in all kinds of jobs. Many Tlingits live in cities in Alaska, Washington, and other states. Others live in small villages as their **ancestors** did. They may know everyone in town. Many Tlingits still hunt and fish for some of their food.

*Tlingits are keeping their traditions alive. These Tlingits are celebrating with the **raven** dance.*

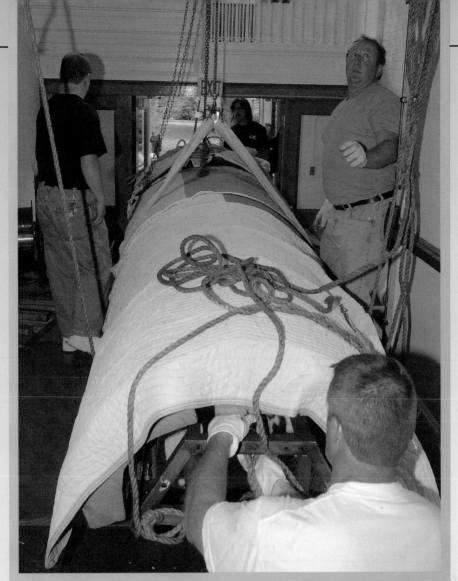

*These men are packing up a **totem pole** at a museum near Boston. It was returned to the Tlingit people in 2001.*

The Tlingit people are passing on their **traditions.**
Tlingit leaders have brought some *at.óow* back to
Alaska from far-away museums. New **carvers** and
weavers are working today. Tlingit children are
learning the Tlingit language. They can go to camps
where they learn about the Tlingit way of life.

The Tlingit Future

Today, many Tlingit children have mixed family backgrounds. They may have a parent or grandparent who is not Tlingit. Tlingit children go to movies, use computers, and ride skateboards. But they are also part of a **clan**. They learn Tlingit **traditions** from their families. They learn to respect the land and the sea. They are Tlingit. They are the future.

Alaskan natives gather for a long weekend every two years. A big parade usually happens on Sunday.

30

Glossary

accent   written mark that means your voice goes higher on that syllable

ancestor   relative who lived long before someone's parents and grandparents

anti-discrimination law   law that says all people must be treated in the same way

boarding school   school where children live

cannery   factory where food is put into cans

canoe   narrow boat pushed along with paddles

carve   cut into a shape with a knife or sharp tool

cedar   large, brown-barked tree that grows in the Pacific Northwest

ceremony   event that celebrates a special occasion

Christian   person who follows a religion based on the teachings of Jesus

clan   group of families that are related

clan symbol   animal or object that stands for a clan

disease   sickness

fort   building with strong walls for defending against an enemy

glacier   large, slow-moving sheet of ice

killer whale   black-and-white whale with teeth

missionary   person who teaches others about religion

moiety   half of the Tlingit tribe

raven   large, black bird

robe   long, loose piece of clothing

settler   person who makes a home in a new place

slave   person who was bought and sold as a worker

spruce   kind of evergreen tree

totem pole   special carving that tells a story or history

tradition   custom or story that has been passed from older people to younger people for a long time

tribe   group of people who share language, customs, beliefs, and often government

weave   lace together threads or other material. A weaving is something made in this way.

More Books to Read

Ansary, Mir Tamim. *Northwest Coast Indians.* Chicago: Heinemann Library, 2000.

Brown, Tricia. *Children of the Midnight Sun: Voices of Alaska's Native Children.* Portland, Ore.: Alaska Northwest Books, 1998.

Staub, Frank J. *Children of the Tlingit.* Minneapolis, Minn.: Carolrhoda Books, 1998.

Index